My Mother is an Old Elephant

Poems
by Peter Neary-Chaplin

My Mother is an Old Elephant
Poems by Peter Neary-Chaplin

First published in 2012 by
Ministry of Words
www.ministryofwords.com

© Peter Neary-Chaplin 2012

The right of Peter Neary-Chaplin to be identified as the author
of this work has been asserted in accordance with sections
77 and 78 of the Copyright, Designs and Patents Act 1988.

A catalogue record for this book
is available from the British Library.

ISBN: 978-0-9574468-0-9

All rights reserved. No part of this publication may
be reproduced, stored in a retrieval system, or
transmitted in any form or by any means, electronic,
mechanical, photocopying, recording, or otherwise,
without the prior permission of the publishers.

Cover design and typesetting by
Steven Levers Publication Design
www.stevenlevers.com

Back cover photography by Ingrid Weel
www.ingridweel.com

This volume is dedicated to the many people who inspired it, directly and indirectly, or jumped through hoops with me during the creation of it, and who listened and helped me to begin to hear my voice, and in particular to my Mum, Josie (who will never get to read it), and to Denise, to Conor and Francesca, and to the faculty, mentors and class of 2011 at the One Spirit Interfaith Foundation (who will). And special thanks to Tom Evans for helping me to find my flame, and to the men of MROP Perth 2010 for helping me to find my gold.

Lots of love to

Malaika

Peter heany chaplm.
(rev!)

xxx

Contents

The man the nurses couldn't catch

Drifting in a lightless undeciding haze,
plodding,
plumping up,
measuring interiors,
dreamless, comfortable,
he missed the path somewhere back aways,
forgot his own advice and took the travelled road.

But now the whale's meandered back
and spat him on a half-remembered track.
In his slippered feet he stands
considering, back and forward,
reckoning by the unrisen sun that rises with his rising sap.

Then, sniffing the warm sea and the light,
gathers his fairweather clothing tight,
slips the comfortable latch,
becomes the man the nurses couldn't catch.

They follow with torches, swarming, pleading, calling,
but he knows how to hide,
nips behind a tree,
dodges grinning in a doorway,
pixellated in party snaps.

What? Those children don't even know his real name.
He is Don Quixote, the Man of La Mancha,
always on the attack,
looking for the one who'll love him back.

10-minute poems

Take a pen
set your minute timer to ten
and catch your words like fleeing dreams,
new butterflies in this child's gentle net
meeting for the first time friend to friend,
already beautifully grown
but not quite finished yet,
still awkward,
still a little wet,
summoned to your party unprepared;
even you don't know what you intend.
And when the clock runs down
stop
ignore
distract
play darts or walk the dog.
Come back tomorrow to redact.
Let today's words
dry in warming sun,
the introductions over,
the hardest part now done.

Keeping the inn at Emmaus

For Adrian Scott

Jesus is up to his games again,
expounding glory on the road,
showing himself in broken hands
breaking new-baked breads,
putting eternal notions into their pulsing heads,
then, over their shoulders,
winking
and vanishing in a pool of light,
leaving them both
blind and with second sight.

I find them stumbling at the wayside,
caught up, mute,
liminal, re-born, motherless.
I take their hands and walk them to the inn,
care for them till retinas heal,
wash dusty robes,
massage exhausted feet,
nurse their apophatic zeal
until they can bear once more to eat,
re-homed by a home-cooked meal.

And when their breathing selves return
their burning hearts begin to speak
while still they burn.
The words emerge with wonder and with pain,
salvations and awakenings,
epiphanies of light,
the loss of all things an overwhelming gain.

And so they warm me at their fire.
I need to hear myself retold
with nods and smiles,
tending my own attenuated flame,
remembering my own warming heart,

wondering why it's not the same
as years ago,
when I too trod those ancient mapless miles,
and everything was crystal clear.
Except where to go from here.

I speak to them of walks,
vigils and retreats,
sacred trees and mass rocks,
of silence, sand and stones,
old sages, older crones,
hospitals and healing pools,
monasteries with spartan rules.

Some spend one night
then go off into all the world
triumphant and refreshed,
their bright apostolic bunting all unfurled.

Others stay too long.
I stitch them into shrouds,
pray over them and put them in the ground
wondering if they should have gone,
moved on
sooner
or made a louder sound.

Not many here tonight.
A face sits by the door, troubled
(they have a certain look)
by something never read in any book.
I'll go and clear his plate
and hope he doesn't want to talk too late.

Under the fig tree

The soil is moist and easy digging
and this corner traps the sun
from noon and through
the day's wane.
I water the root ball of my new fig tree,
heel it in and settle the spoil.
When I've had some lunch
and washed up a bit
I'm going out there to sit
until I hear
loud and clear,
until I'm seen
like that old Israelite who had no guile,
who sat and cooled his feet
took shade and spoke his charmless mind,
mission-blind.
And I shall speak my own
and shall not care
how great a burden I'll be asked to bear.

And so I sat,
squeezed in under baby branches,
huddled up, hunched,
practising my protestant zen.
I stayed till ten
when it rained again.
My back got sore.
I couldn't sit there any more.

The first weeks were a salutary discipline,
a sinking down,
a weathering in,
a gathering order in the indented ground.
The wakening stems eased out
without a sound.

That was thirty years ago
and still sometimes I sit out there
though nowadays I take a chair.
No voice descended from the sky,
no great platform opened up,
no air tickets in the mail,
no desperate begging letters from afar.
Just regular commuting in the car.

One balmy day the fig tree tapped my shoulder,
had a quiet word, or two
as I stretched out among its arms.
"Bear fruit," it sighed.
"Is that it?" I replied
as the saviour in me died.

After that I ate the figs
and shared them with whoever came.
We talked in parables,
of other lives and ours.
I wrote words, we drank cold beer.
We listened and we learned to hear
and sat content,
our feet among the flowers.

Panning for gold

He rises early most days,
the curve of dawn
seamlessly surfing the breathing bubble
that brings him up from his river bed
of smiling slumber
and beaches him
wet-booted
on the shallow dirt bank of the surging stream
that's just an armspan
too wide for a man.

Bright-winged birds agree in flashing song,
the sun is up onto its knees.

Coffee warms his fingers
round the jagged pan.
He ponders where to start,
to look, to listen
for the tinkling rhythms of the day
in the river's clue.

Some days a nugget comes
to feed him or fix his teeth
but he would pan anyway,
this his joyful doing.
The swirl of gravel and the rusty metal
in his cupped and cankered hands
are exhausted wedding flagons
charged
with bone-icing new water
that turns into golden wine
at his obedience.

My mother is an old elephant

Some days
when hair is freshly washed,
she sits unpermed,
no longer ageing,
like a great-great-grandmother.
Nose and cheekbones tighten
her transparent skin,
preparing it for the lessening of death,
for the underglow
the composting fire of union.

Other days she breathes out song with her whole softened
body,
wordless and exact
freed of thought
effortless
as if slapping wet clothing on some river's rock,
and wanders smiling through meadows of memory
with Wesley and Purcell.

But there are days when
close up
her eye is the eye of an old elephant
that sees the limitless grassland around her
and sways,
a mitochondrial mammoth who ever knew
that the field beyond right and wrong was always here
under our feet
and we have lived in it,
not believing
that the only sin was to withhold,
and here she is
blessing still,
but all poured out,
all overflowed,
her story told.

The understudy

Every now and again
when the worship of the heaving crowd
and their violent adoration
becomes too loud,
as if to carry him off
overhead down the dusty street
and out of sight
to his own breast-beating funeral rite,
his foundation starts to crumble,
the eye liner starts to sting,
his costume pinches
and the brilliantly drawn character
lit up by ego and long scotches
in, frankly, dim and inadequate dressing rooms,
quakes,
the strain of constant excellence begins to tell,
the pain of leadership stoops
his broad Shakespearean frame,
his ears begin to ring,
his pulse booms,
some dark thing looms
that even whisky cannot quell.
Ladies and gentlemen,
the actor is unwell.

And so steps up a quieter man
to stand before the baying stalls.
Looks the same
if a little smaller, less made up,
less vain.
Plays the role a little more sober,
more contained, less pained.
Disappointing, doesn't have the balls,
the critics say.
And so the people stay away.

Yet some are drawn
by less clamour and less scorn.
They hear a subtler tone
perhaps more like their own.
And at the curtain
they don't set sail for local wine bars
noising their knowledgeable distaste,
protesting, short-changed,
but remain seated awhile
then gather in a loose, shy knot
at the stage door,
staying to thank the understudy
who wove a story they'd never heard before.

Slow revelation

These days revelation comes slow
seeming less to strike
and more to grow.
The temple curtain is no longer ripped
from top to floor
but unravels and frays
decays a little more
with the accelerating days.

And God
speaks less in strident tone
retreating to the substrate,
perhaps preferring time alone
with the odd centenarian whisper
or low groan,
hiding herself again
from the cooling passion of my hunt;
my meanings were like missile attacks;
her answers, now less storied,
are delegated,
spoken in a pattern of crazed luciferous cracks
revealing just the uncreated glow,
an undergound lighthouse
on the wrecking rock
to which the winds of her breath blow.

Bolts of lightning

I have prayed for miracles,
revelations,
incontrovertible proofs,
stared flat-kneed at the candle,
witnessed it drip, droop and flow
down to a floor-pool,
picked blackened match heads
out of its clear white flesh,
leaving fingerprint whorls
in case the ageing sky-god
has forgotten
who it is that calls.

Once a bolt of lightning
arced down from the dark,
blasted a tiny crack
in the ground nearby
showing where to dig
but not why.

Some stringless kite

When I am dead
and breath no longer kisses my red
blood, and I am bled,
put this clay back whence it came
with its chequer board
of glory and of shame,
perfect now and without blame.

Then like some stringless kite I'll flutter up,
unhurried in the tall air,
no need to be in service any more,
no anchor anywhere,
unharnessed,
moorings slipped,
freed upon the wind
to butterfly and play
around the empty sky.

When that day comes, look up
and stupefy
until another child of God,
another innocent walks by
and calls you out by name,
needing a bed,
a cut of bread,
offering another love that must be fed.

Take that hand
and watch the kite get small.
It cannot fall,
its duty is to fly.
Yours, to let it go,
to see inside another eye
my mirrored kite
with fresh unburdened sight
that I
shall bless with what remains of all my might.

The monk's hair

Why does he shave his noble head?
Does hair mean wild and none mean tame?
May he not grow his mane instead?
Could Brother Legion be his name?

And did not God make every beast
Including this green, bear-like priest
Who kills and eats and mates and prays,
Whom sunset and sunrise amaze?

But all of him is for the fire
Prayer-book, ribcage, hair and stole.
He yields himself to what consumes
Becoming flame, becoming whole.

Sons and fathers

I met a soldier on the road
that led down from the frozen loch.
My face shrieked with the tortured load
of my communion with cold rock.
We walked along and talked of things
that started down in meat and bone
then rose through filters of the mind.
I owned the shock that was my own
and wasn't wrong and wasn't right.
It forced its proper way outside
in hacking grief and fists held tight.
He spoke of killings unresolved,
of dreams that would not go away,
of taint and guilt in young men's minds
and memories that came to stay.
And as we spoke and rain came down
I felt the presence of some plan.
My pulses cooled, my fists unwound.
The son was father to the man.

Sadhu and the flat rock

Sadhu sits
still
on a flat rock made just for his bones,
breathes his belly out
and waits until he can hear the upseeping sap
in the legs of the forest.
'Make a eucharist for my children,' says the flat rock.
Sadhu jumps down like a boy,
breaks a loaf and scatters it.
'Both loaves.'
Sadhu smiles, breaks his last loaf.
I have no wine, he thinks.
'You are not looking,' says the rock.
He gathers blackberries,
squeezes them into a small smooth hollow.

Sadhu sits,
the afternoon eternal.
Sparrows, mice, ants come
pecking, nibbling, carrying away the crumbs,
wasps hover over the stickening juice.
As the sun's tap closes and the light pools,
deer loom not far off,
mosquitoes gather round their warmth,
bats and foxes stretch.

Dusk pangs move Sadhu on, and in his way
are pignuts, wild garlic, and leaves of bitter elm
who also listened for the flat rock's voice.

The old man and the yew tree

The world's run out of wisdom,
building roads where no cities are
and praying for traffic and pastry sales,
accelerating the tow of stupid seeds in hot exhausts.
But the soul still travels overland,
over sand,
at the speed of a camel,
and when you're older
and the glassy-eyed twitching has stopped,
you'll regret the cutting of the old yew tree
that needed you
even less than you needed me.

Does my foot know it's Monday?

Lumpen, silty stirring
around the tremulous half-buried flat fins,
elegant eddies of waste, waltzing.
No-one can see me down here
quilted by fine sand, camouflaged.
Think I might stay.
Haven't been a fish before, soft warm stomach-sleeping.
Now a filament of sand glides by
down and left,
in and out between green fronds
abrading, nibbling at flakes of skin
between yellowing toes.
Toes?

Watery dawn rays play on feet cold
from uncovering,
tingled by the sunlight
and sending a slow signal up the long drowsy tracks
towards the capital,
where feet have heeled shoes.
Does my foot know it's Monday?
I was happier as a fish.

Unorthodox priest

When God's white eye lifts slowly in the east
and heats to vapour the swollen millrace of dreams
that call the priest
awake and up and into dazed attention,
and thankfulness arises in his heart
for light and warmth
and all the teeming stuff of earthy life
that comes with just a little tilling
and ancestral knowing of the place,
the woodpecker his alarm,
the timid deer his wife,
then he knows no better way to start
than touching forehead to the ground
and painting blessing
in every chamber of his heart
so that it leaks a bit with every beat
and blesses every tiny space
just like the worms beneath his feet.

Young rage

I have a mongrel pup
called rage.
Always tightly held,
not allowed to age,
never growing up.
And now I've let him off the leash
to race around like mad,
flattened ears,
noisy, troublesome, lost,
barking at stupid drivers,
stupid shoppers,
litter louts,
bad pavement manners,
the ten o'clock news,
advertising banners.
When he's older he'll bark less,
maybe bare his teeth and grumble,
recognizing friends and boundaries,
not so spooked by hedgerow rustles,
better schooled by rough and tumble.
But just now he needs to run
and run
and as he runs he grows,
throws himself into soft-muscled twitching sleep
where he leaps with butterflies, bees and bitches,
chasing and biting
whatever touches eye or nose.

Meditate like an oyster

I went down to the shoreline
to listen to my father's advice.
He was out, at work I guessed.
Perhaps he meant that for the best,
but he had left a note
taped to the hull of his boat.
Our boat.

Meditate like an oyster, it read.
No armchair, no straightened spine,
no emptying, no depth of breath, no Zen.
Arch your back, hunker down,
small and sealed against it all
except the tear that rises from your deep shinbone marrow,
and the friendly grain of sand,
then rock and rock with the belly-hammering tide.
Sleep there until your raspberry eyes begin to soften.
For all things are possible
but some things are written:
snot, pearls,
other worlds.

Bury me under a tree

Bury me under a tree
then I may feed the earth that nourished me.

Sow lilies round my feet
so as their journey ends they may once more smell sweet.

Beside my hands grow maize.
Feed children on the labour of my days.

Upon my head put sage
the mark of wisdom's dawning in old age.

Plant on my heart the burning bush of old.
Consuming fire consumed, and turned to gold.

Bury me under a tree.
The life I owe I now give back to thee.

First light

First light, and I revisit the wasteland
Uncovering the clumsy hooligan's mess.
He's been blundering around again,
his big drunken feet trampling the flowers,
his empty cans mourning and clanking.

I fill in the kicked divots
dragging aside the lame shopping trolleys
the dumb fridges,
raking, sweeping, making straight,
till the heart's eye conjures the garden again
and at the centre a laid table, lit with golden edges
in the presence of the mundane.

Here I can sit
and point my silver-pointed mind down
into deeper reaches
where there's no grip, no morning,
the sign seen only by those who wait

The boatweaver

The boatweaver padded early to the river bank,
sat and listened to the slow, fat ooze
till the detail filtered through that he could use.
Not name, not face, not colour,
nor Hebrew race,
just size and weight and time and landing place.
Then, checking left and right, he realised his task,
what he would need
to find, inspect, to cut and clean the reed,
measure, trim, weave and seal,
his fast hand fashioning a smaller, faster craft
to take today's child out to where the flow has its fastest feel,
swooping past the regal shore
where gentle ladies bathe on a gentle slope,
avoiding Pharaoh's haughty, painted wife
who, even so,
knew more of life
than her husband's or some doctor's knife,
round to the rougher, steeper, working waters
where raw-handed women beat the family clothes,
and childless mothers keep a sharp watch for woven boats,
and hope.

Balaam

I rest under no roof.
I am the dusty traveller,
the journey, the road,
the pothole and the hoof.

I am Balaam and the voice I hear
is my breathing creature
plodding on,
eating straw,
seeing angels.

Yesterday

I have buried yesterday
beneath a grieving loam,
sat pondering its epitaph,
how to mark its passing,
how to make it feel like home.

Tomorrow I'll dig again,
and do the same thing with today
if God grants me my spade and strength.
And tomorrow will become just another place I used to live.
Today, though, is like a small shy bird,
a fluttering wren
that might just come to me when
I learn to ask well.
And the question is,
What is the question?

Pieces

I am in a thousand small pieces
like the glass that protected
the image of the holy family
or the amber glaze of a romantic old master.
And now the light refracts through me
into mud red and blood blue,
purpling the earth,
but the white
the silver
the gold
are gone.

Death needs softer ground

Didn't think it was so far down, nor so quick,
mistaking my altitude.
Not the grainy, polished granite of graves
where I listen for my fathers
and hear my voice's echo on the loving letters
that generations of gruff, black-handed masons
magic out of the earth's cooling core.

They know more of stone than I,
my spine arched over streaming, shattered needles
where there is no further to fall,
the bedrock, the ground of being,
the end of plans.

There is no bed here, no sleep,
no dust or ash, no death.
Death needs softer ground
and here the name my father gave
becomes its own gift to me,
whispers of a foothold big enough to stand on
and raise my vertical head to face
the relentless granite of continuing.

Prayer closet

Drawn down a narrow, curved stair
below the working life of a peopled day
I found a never-opened door,
unlocked, it turned out,
waiting windowless,
empty, cool and unexamined.

So I closed my eyes and sat
since nothing seemed worth looking at
and, feeling holy, prayed
with half a heart, for this, for that.

Then nothing was in my head
but purring wings over sedimenting silence,
the steady tide of undemanding breath,
desire's easy death.

Soon I looked up again
and saw a bright, tiny window
that wasn't there when
this time,
this interval,
this universe began.

Crossing thresholds

In all your time and mine,
in the smiling soul's heat and the glacial lack,
sun-soaked days and black,
when delight ran round our lips and spilled like juice,
when sadness hung around us like a noose
we opened up like flowers and sidled together
avoiding too much of the look,
preferred meandering and making spirals,
walking backwards,
bumping shoulders,
hands in pockets, shields down, scanning.

Until at some point we always reached a crossing, from trail
to none,
into the holiest of the wild ground
where the next step had no warranty and no recourse
where the fig trees grew no leaves.

I took one more step
and called you in.
You never came
refusing to be known,
withholding the best and last,
the ungovernable,
inchoate glory, dark-glassed.

Why so scared?
There was only you and I
and I am no angry God.

My left leg

I was born two-named, two-legged,
right and left,
two-storied, double-clanned.
Narrow-road brethren seeded loose-wheeled lightfoots
and, in the way of things,
her name surrendered
proud and ashamed of the good trade that took place,
and ran away to the tall timber.

The righteous won, pinched, proper, civic, good people, hard
and strong,
and the men ministered their consent
praying hard, well-meant
against the forgiving cussedness,
the golden, the female,
the drinking, warm and feckless,
two different glories, neither shining.

So I unpray that guillotining prayer
and welcome back my other timid name
as an honoured equal to the fire,
where we will speak of other stories,
other people, other gods,
my left leg still sound
and pounding the ground with a belonging beat.

Answered prayer

Reaching the end of the lumpy, mired road, you tend to
wait.
Years, sometimes.
A decade, more.
A decade of waiting.
Of anguished soulscreech,
superheated tears,
cracked elbows on the waxy altar rail,
dessicated supplications,
dry and white like old soldiers' bones
that crumble and blow around, evaporating.

But you find no answer on a fusty hassock,
on your broken knees,
just that long, slow, returning echo
that fixes your distance,
how far away you are.

And, after the night whose minutes are longer than months
comes the dawning of a careless permission
to stand once again, hind-legged in the reflecting gaze of
heaven,
feeling the muscles of movement gather.

For all your holy waiting, your body knew more than you,
and now begins to test its coils
feeling the wind lift,
the season change
and the mud harden again into a road.
And the answer comes
only and truly when flesh and sinew tighten,
a blistered heel presses against the ruts
and a new land falls under the sole of your moving foot.

Godspeed with a happy sound

Do you remember
when storms threw trees across the hospital road,
when we stood in wet cemeteries,
signed papers with trembling hands,
when surgeons dragged our glorious, bloody children
to wide-eyed, fascinating life,
when the view of the reeks opened wide and sunny on
charmed summer days
and we sang our songs
and roared approval of the others', full-hearted, full-bellied?

In my deep knowing parts I know that I was not so bad.
Perhaps we both deserved a fairer judge.

But though it fall as dry powder to the ground
I shall bless and decree
godspeed with a happy sound.

Woven

I am
woven in
to a fabric designed in a far-off croft
by a woman (or a man) I don't remember meeting
until maybe just now
as a sun flash echoed on a silver thread that felt familial
and sent a pulse across the warp
that tickled my feet awake
and sprayed a hologram aloft
where all things were my cousins, more or less,
and the one saying I am
had no edge, no name, no mission,
just played with patterns in the light.

This livelong day

I love you enough
to give you back this livelong day,
just dawned,
fat and soft and fresh like a peach,
unrobed and pregnant,

to wait on you for the marrow
that springs and warms and cleans my rushing blood,
to hand out freely the salt and sweet,
the rising yeast, my bread and meat
which were not ever mine but only lent
to test how bounty might be spent,

to withhold the bitter and the sour,
cook them slowly for an hour,
find their place,
discern their power.

Shall I learn today?
Shall I teach?
Both are one,
and balance is only ever stumbled upon
as I dance lightly on my beautiful feet
to God only knows where.

Healing waters

An angel stirred up the pool at noon
one bleak brown day in winter.
We dragged ourselves up,
on haunches, on crutches,
on brittle bones, on pressed pills and radium rays,
not racing any more these days,
preferring this half-dead unhealing,
so old we can finger only scars.
And no luck again today, nor soon.

But, as I sink back out of hope,
father's spirit gathers from the lucid lime-bright water,
rises like steam, coalesces towards me,
drags over the waters,
commands ordered columns from the shapeless vapour,
arms flung extravagantly wide,
forgives my sin,
softly seeping through my broken skin.

Fly fishing

On the curling bank
where the kingfisher's branch lowers over the slow pool
the old man sits for centuries
nursing his line
patiently possessing his soul,
dreaming, waiting,

for this gorgeous yellow-silver bream
twisting, flashing, strong,
made clever by other hooks
and not knowing his gentle hand
would only stroke her
and set her free.

Paddy's Gone to Istanbul

For (and about) Ges Armor

Paddy's done his normal trick,
given my face a long, hard lick
and legged it.
From a mad wet pup he was away to the bins
or the kids on the swings
or the landlady's boss-eyed pug
wafting her love round the houses
and Paddy towering over her
wagging hard and ready for anything.
Or the pub
where daft blokes gave him ale
and shouted get home lad, yer under age, ha ha.
And then he'd sleep
toddling home in the midnight
whimpering and smelling of dug drains.
He might come, if you shouted loud and the wind was right.
He might.
The trips got grander as he grew
from smaller town to bigger town,
the soul of a poet
with the head of a clown.
But now he's done it.
Gone to Istanbul it seems
one day when the wind changed.
Some sassy Turkish bitch, no doubt,
but the art and the culture really do stand out.
So we'll still adore him, and him us
when he wanders back this way.
But we've a labrador now too
in case we never see that day.

Secret agent

I am a secret agent,
been so since I was eight.
I have a special mission,
a special, dangerous fate.
There's stuff that I can't talk about
as careless talk costs lives.
I've never told my best friend Jack,
nor either of my wives.
My kids just think I'm barmy
so my cover's holding well.
They come and visit once a month
but still I will not tell.
A secret agent must be smart,
remain one step ahead,
so when they think they've got it,
it's really something else instead.
I think I'm called a sleeper,
a man who's lying low.
Appearances are normal,
no fuss or noise or show.
And none around would ever guess
the secret that I hold.
I eat and drink and pray and bless
and steadily grow old.
I'll have my moment. When it's time
a signal will arrive.
I haven't had my orders yet
though I'm now eighty-five.
So waiting seems to be for now
the only thing to do.
We secret agents never know
the when, the where, the who.
And maybe I have colleagues
who are also keeping mum.
That might explain their knowing smiles
and equilibrium.

Perhaps at my memorial
when I'm no longer here
a coded message will come through
for someone I hold dear.
A verse from Psalms or gospels,
a text on polished stone,
a cryptic comment from the priest,
a word carelessly sown.
And then I shall be smiling,
my mission finally done,
Some warrior shall inherit
my agent's unfired gun,
and hide it in their holster
and know their special role
is to be a secret agent
at the centre of their soul.

Strange disciple

Held no creed
believed in what he could believe
bending like a flaxen reed.
Blessing where blessing lacked
healed heavy souls and broken-backed.
Never knew the master's gaze,
fought with his men
who thought they had the rights back then
not recognising whom they praised.

Spent his long days doing good
caring, mending, defending
putting heart in heartless places
winning some, losing more
never keeping score.

Now buried with a single stone
by half-men from among the tombs
who knew a saint by smell alone
and waited for the carnival to leave
then carved his name and beat their breast
full men at their very best.

Who was that man, he'd often thought
who threw the fire that he had caught?

Loving this woman

Loving this woman has two sounds.
One, high in the fast air,
played on a singing filament
scarcely heard
until the clear wind brings her to me,
buffeting my ears between slivers of whispered spirit.

The other a pounding drum
heard through her perfumed ribs and mine,
through debts and blood and fights,
through straps and lace,
long-kissed lips,
and ancient meanings in her face.

Beeline

Swinging round the sunny dahlias,
cresting a white river of air along the border's edge
it dives into an eddy,
probing the anagallis,
hovers,
then plunges headfirst-heedless
into the open blue trumpet,
arse up,
fine-whiskered legs scrambling,
pressing hard into the lemon-yellow dust.
Silent baby sucks,
a short, sated somnolence.
Then a rough shove
out again
into the current and on.

Sweet peas

Slashed silk splaying,
flamenco style
in a tremor of hot evening air,
wine-dark, satin-white, cobalt,
their clean curved edges swivel like blades
and rest, still open, panting,
proud as real women.

Brighstone Bay, IoW

On the flyblown, sandy clifftop
the day's hard, steady blast squeezed us through
the vaulted dusk and made us mad,
hissing like a closing valve,
and stiffened the prancing water
into dull elephant hide
that crept forward,
crept back
forward
back
mesmerized
by the white butter moon.

Low water

In the harbour's pewter silence
the leaden, weed-draped mooring rope
drips into rutted, stinking mud,
dead, and bled of blessing,
dirty sand and bladderwrack.
My dry sagging hulk wants a lick of paint
but craves with unscrambled purity
the turning and returning of the sea
that even the scrapping gulls lack.

But this is a waiting older than sponge,
a lusting known
deep in the cells of wood and stone.

The field at Ballaghboy

Before the track makes Dursey
you find a tidy green field,
upland against rocks,
cambered to catch the slanting sun
where straggling, dirty sheep
drift disorderly,
distant at the edge of the gale
like foam at the top of the strand,
straining headstrong across the long curving combed mounds
where the fevered tubers caught the rot.
This neat, sad, loyal tending
even the grinding salty air does not kill.

Navigating

Show me how beauty is made.
The working of word and stone,
the universe's massive swing,
creaking rhubarb and a soft, fallow deer,
the unhedged meadow where they grow.

The scalpel violin,
the vat of musty wine
the smell of women and of wood.

Does beauty make itself again through me?
I hope,
and line my compass with its north
to test the map I drew against its pole,
taking bearings as I go,
aiming straight
and calculating for the undertow.

The contents of my head

Where do they stop and start,
the contents of my head?
How do they flow in and out?
Through holes, like rain,
through bone, like waves?
Perhaps they huddle,
desolate in an upper room,
grieving disciples,
waiting for Jesus to come among them
and usher them smiling out,
fresh, blinded, stumbling
into the testing world
where they might be weak,
might fail, or die,
burn under a hostile glass,
or melt or crack ice
with their infant fingers of purple flame,
watering the ground.

Clay man

Spent in a long landscape,
My sickness and I weathered
At the foot of tall splintered crags
Where killing birds nest and the metal day drags.

No forward step, no hearty friend,
No fellow traveller heaven-sent,
No hearth or kiss.
Just cold brush, a starry sky
And the blue night's murderous lament.

And my stone-frozen back hardens round the hard ground,
Congeals around its jagged edge.
I am its stolen rib.
We were clay together at the start,
Lay together side by side
Before science, before sin,
When everyone could enter in.

White night

I nail my stare upon the moon
The grass and treetops seeping by
Mist meanders round the lake
Its waters gather in my eye
My thinking spark fades down to brown
All higher functions now are gone
The reptile's keeping me awake.

The ark came to my house

The ark came to my house.
Four dark-muscled men, steaming with sweat
knocked and entered, by command they said.
No need to sign, we know who you are,
searched for a safe corner.
Safe, they said, in voices like lead,
you understand.
Took one last look,
the husked and grainy linen cloth spread across,
gathered, tied.

No-one came back.
My hair grew black
and thicker than before
my wedding day
when all the world stood ready in the atom gap.
And all I would have wished seemed once more ready to
uncloak.
But long-held lust gets whittled down the years
and blessing changes for a canny bloke.
And the ark, undisturbed, abides
and wafts a birthing pheromone about.
Some humbler enterprise awaits its day,
like a father's late-born child
loved hard because the time is less,
a life of love contained in its compress.

Let me go grey again to work this extra gift
until its end.
This is time that I will gladly spend.

I've always been fifty-one

I've always been fifty-one.
The thought just stabbed me
Like a hypodermic, spreading a cool familiar fluid
Through the crimpling skin
Where head and neck dispute the boundaries.

I know it now though.
The middle-aged, out of place
weariness at fifteen
definitively mine, no question.
But from this quieter, slowing future
uneasy with the youthful surging chaos,
blazers, bags, books,
skipped meals, shaving cuts,
knowing always when too far had come
I slipped out of shameful capture's way.
Hearing of an older person's death,
always going to the grave,
carrying something not yet due.

So this is what that ancient feeling was,
a premonition from the man.
The youngster grew up partly old
if he grew up at all,
and decodes the plangent echo better
now it bounces back off its own younger face
coming to rest in a more rightful place.

Self-defence

Under my sweating back,
green-eyed, wild,
heaving hot, meaty breath,
needle claws arc deep down
into my punctured shoulders,
my ripped leg flesh.
But two belly stabs
of a poised blade
have stretched out a long space in its dying.
So I shiver while a pearl wall clouds its eyes.
Don't move.
Killing is slow, not sudden, for him and for me,
And we are closer than skin.
So I must learn to bleed, breathe, wait.

A Lenten fast

I've given up thinking for Lent.
Too much energy
has been spent
on that word 'thought'
which always seems to come up
short.

Crazed northern lights
are jazzing in my head
made mad by solar flares
and dancing like spring hares
their eyes and blood all red.

I'm just going to sit and watch the show
and care not to know
why there's this titanic tug
between my little leaping mind
and that performing sky.
I shall just see
and feel
and be
and clap my grizzled hands
with childlike glee.

Waiting room

Dying is a long thing,
a million bright moments carefully collected like stamps,
pressed between powdery pages,
an uncurated gospel of fragments.
Interpretation comes only
with the final part.
For now, we hold skinny hands in this waiting room.
The mattress pump purrs.
I witness every flicker of her alabaster face,
and dream of returning to memories of days with heart,
knowing that this book must close
and another life for each must start
with her repose.

Prayer beads

This one's for the Hindu
This one's for the monk
This one's for the amma
Sleeping on her sandstone bunk

This one's for the healer
This one's for the nun
This one's for the zealot
For whom enough was never was done

This one's for the imam
This one's for the Jew
This one's for the druid
Who still prays beneath the yew

This one's for the Buddhist
This one's for the Jain
This one's for all those
Who'll come back time and time again

This one's for the Christian
This one's for the Sikh
This one's for the listeners
Who let the other speak

This one's for the atheist
Who celebrates this life
This one's for the bigot
Whose prayer cuts like a knife

This one's for the majesty
Enrobed in fire and smoke
This one's for the timid boy
Whose spirit never spoke

This one's for the future
Which happened years ago
This one's for the present
Where I stand in the flow

The Isaac knife

Sitting orderly
square-shouldered, solid, tidy, fat
atop this table
of sacrifice
I throw a shy uncertain light,
and ask, who put the match to me
and placed me here
in this cool symmetry
and made me nice
enough to draw you to your steady uncomplaining penance,
witnessing your bent knees
your increments of contrition?

But I desire
to grip this altar's Isaac knife
and cut my frame
repenting deep and true,
and open up a channel,
let the fusty air rush in
and safety all flow out,
and watch my flame leap all about,
spit and tremble
and burn your eye
and start to melt from deep within my heart,
to sit between lovers
of wine and curling smoke
on red and white tablecloths,
throwing deep and dancing shadows behind better sins,
the ones that open you up wide
like this my open side
where I have lost control,
given myself to air and flow and flame,
joined in the game,
letting in wild fire
among the tame.

Visiting Mum

She lies down all the time now,
turned by kind hands,
living in the space
between her face
and this plain wall,
sometimes understanding
I'm here beside,
other times dispersed
among the floating radio waves,
out upon the voiceless tide.
With each ebb the angels keep a little more.
With each flow, a little less returns to shore.

Little funeral

This is a fine hole, small and neat.
I took my time, no hurry now.
Perhaps a bit more square
than might have suited you
whom I never knew
for whom there was no chance to care.

The earth gave way with grace
seeing the shadows lengthen on my face
because I had no scrap of you to place.

So I adopt you as my own
lend you my clothes of flesh and bone,
turning once your unturned stone,
and now declare that you
incarnate
came to pass
were seen
were blessed
were named
took part,
that your third father, unashamed,
found space within his heart
to dig for you this little grave,
to put you back with smiles
beneath this breathing emerald grass.

About the author

Peter Neary-Chaplin is something of a mongrel. At various times throughout a variegated, not to say chequered career, he has been a Cambridge open scholar, warehouseman, cocktail barman, project manager, roadie, copywriter, amateur actor, bus driver, timeshare hawker (fail), publisher, advertising salesman,  spiritual counsellor, musician, internet marketer, volunteer hospice chaplain, interfaith minister, worship leader, information developer and IT trainer, pub manager, freelance journalist, husband (fail), kibbutznik and farm labourer, and he remains, in addition to some of these, a proud Dad, a film-lover, wine-bibber, initiated man, amateur theologian (fail), free-thinker, wedding and funeral celebrant, author and poet, who takes at face value the biblical example of hanging around with publicans and sinners.

He lives in Surrey, England, the last place on earth he ever thought he'd end up, and cheers himself up by digging escape tunnels to Lord only knows where.

17356173R10036

Made in the USA
Charleston, SC
07 February 2013